HOMELESS IN AMERICA

HOMELESS IN AMERICA

a joint project of

THE NATIONAL MENTAL HEALTH ASSOCIATION
and

FAMILIES FOR THE HOMELESS
(a non-partisan coalition of
congressional, administration and media families)

ACROPOLIS BOOKS
WASHINGTON, DC

Editor: MICHAEL A.W. EVANS

Associate Editor: MARJORIE BROWN

Assistant Editor: KATHERINE GLENNON

Contract Photographers:

MARY ELLEN MARK   EUGENE RICHARDS

WILLIAM PIERCE   STEPHEN SHAMES

ELI REED

Consultant & Photographer: JIM HUBBARD

Contributing Photographers:

GEORGE COHEN   MICHAEL JOHNSON

JAMES CONROY   ROBB KENDRICK

RONALD CORBIN   ABRAHAM MENASHE

NANCY MILLER ELLIOTT   RAY MORTENSON

PHIL FARNSWORTH   MICHAEL O'BRIEN

MAUREEN FENNELLI   WILLIAM VIGGIANO

EVE FOWLER   KIM WEIMER

JEROME FRIAR   DON WEINSTEIN

TONEE HARBERT   GRACE WOJDA

Intern Photographers:

D. KEVIN ELLIOTT   AKEMI MIYAMA

SIBYLLA HERBRICH   GARY POWELL

AXEL KOESTER   CINDY WEINSTOCK

LOUP LANGTON

Counsel: PHILIP HORTON
Arnold & Porter

Public Relations: STORY SHEM & MARTHENA COWART
ARRIVE Unlimited, Inc.

Curatorial Advisor: JANE LIVINGSTON
Associate Director and Chief Curator
Corcoran Gallery of Art

Writer: DUDLEY CLENDINEN
Assistant Managing Editor for Features
The Atlanta Journal & The Atlanta Constitution

Consultant/Photo Editing:
CAROLE GREENAWALT MCKAY
Photo Editor
The White House

Editorial Consultant: IRV MOLOTSKY
The New York Times/Washington Bureau

Book and Exhibition Designers:
CASTRO/HOLLOWPRESS

Printer of Photography: AMY R. WHITESIDE

Video Producer: ROBIN SMITH

Traveling Exhibition Consultant:
LISA CREMIN & ASSOCIATES,
New York

Cover photograph: Mary Ellen Mark; *Back cover photograph:* Robb Kendrick; *Frontispiece:* Gary Powell

Published by
ACROPOLIS BOOKS LTD.
Colortone Building, 2400 17th Street, N.W.
Washington, D.C. 20009

Printed in the United States of America by
COLORTONE PRESS
Creative Graphics, Inc.
Washington, D.C. 20009

The Library of Congress Cataloging in Publication Data
> Homeless in America
> "A Joint Project of National Mental Association & Families for the Homeless."
> Includes Index.
> 1. Homelessness—United States.
> 2. Homelessness—United States—Pictorial Work.
> 3. Homeless persons—United States.
> 4. Homeless persons—United States—Pictorial Work.
I Evans, Michael, 1944–
II National Mental Health Association (U.S.).
III Families for the Homeless (group).
IV Title. H.V. 4505. H652 1988 262.5'0973 88-3486.
ISBN No. 0-87491-888-X. ISBN 0-87491-905-5 (pbk).

CONTENTS

Principal funding for

HOMELESS IN AMERICA: A PHOTOGRAPHIC PROJECT
was provided by

TRIANGLE INDUSTRIES, INC.

with additional generous grants from

EASTMAN KODAK COMPANY
PUBLIC WELFARE FOUNDATION
FEDERAL NATIONAL MORTGAGE ASSOCIATION FOUNDATION
(FANNIE MAE)

Royalties from the sale of HOMELESS IN AMERICA will be shared among creative contributors to the book and the National Mental Health Association's Homeless in America Fund.

This book is witness to the range of Americans who have no place to live.

We all have names for them — street people, bag ladies, bums, winos — but they are so much more than that. They have their own names and feelings and hopes and fears, just like the rest of us. Today families represent the fastest growing segment of this population.

People are becoming homeless at an alarming rate, for a wide variety of reasons, making it clear that the roots of homelessness in America lie in the very structure of our economic and social service systems.

We call upon all Americans to share our outrage at the very existence of homelessness in this country, and to take action. All of us — individuals, corporations, government agencies, churches and synagogues — must join in an alliance to solve this problem, united by the conviction that homelessness is unacceptable.

The night before we wrote this message, two children were stabbed to death in a shelter in Washington, D.C. They were not alcoholics. They were not drug addicts. They were not homeless by choice. They simply had nowhere else to go.

We must not let homelessness become an American institution.

> — THE GOVERNING BOARD,
>   HOMELESS IN AMERICA: A PHOTOGRAPHIC PROJECT

Overleaf:
One of thousands of vacant buildings across the United States.
South Bronx, New York July 1985
RAY MORTENSON

Life in the woods of Naples, Florida. Many men camped here are Viet Nam Veterans,
day laborers who find housing in Naples unaffordable.
August 1987
EUGENE RICHARDS

THE PROBLEM

In the splendid warmth of June, in Washington, Congress authorized $443-million in new aid for the nation's homeless for the balance of the year.

In the last week of October, with the weather still mild, the city government of New York began picking up and hospitalizing homeless people who showed signs of severe mental illness, to get them off the streets. And then in the first week of November, Friday turned grey and sharp and cold. The winter season had begun, threatening the lives of the sort of people pictured in this book.

On the Lower East Side of New York that bitter day, two barrels stood in the bleak expanse of Tomkins Square Park. A fire muttered in the bottom of each, and damaged men held their hands to the warmth. At the first barrel, feeding a scavenged store of wooden coathangers to the flames, stood Jimmy-the-Indian as he called himself. "Where do I live? On this bench," he said. "I'm the only Indian left. The rest of them died."

At the second barrel, the men were burning books. The smoke eddied out and whipped away on the wind as Laura Santiago approached them to compare experiences. She told them that she was homeless, too. She had had her fill of the city's crowded, chaotic emergency shelters, and its violent welfare hotels. She hated them. She and her husband and little boy had found sanctuary in an abandoned building, and there they would pass the winter.

One of the men spoke up. "I was born in East New York. I'm 29," Daniel Ortiz said. He wore a glazed expression in a swollen face. He had had two marriages, he said, and three children. "I've only been out here about four months. I had a problem with my wife. Now I stay here. I used to live in Brooklyn. I was in love," he said sadly. "It broke my heart."

He was holding a shopping cart loosely piled with books, fuel for the flames. Mrs. Santiago watched him stir the surface of the pile with one hand. He pushed aside *A Practical Introduction to Business* and the *Fall, 1987, Sampler from a Mysterious Press*, poking in the middle.

"You don't believe in shelters, either, do you?" she said. He paused, staring at *Being There* by Jerzy Kozinski, and *All Creatures Great and Small,* by James Herriot. "No," he said. "I'm against

Dudley Clendinen is Assistant Managing Editor for Features at *The Atlanta Journal* and *The Atlanta Constitution.* He was National Correspondent for *The New York Times.*

them." There was another pause. "My parents wanted me to go to Puerto Rico with them, but I said I had to take care of my own self."

He fell silent again. As Mrs. Santiago walked away, Daniel Ortiz was blinking uncertainly at *Who Shall Live: Health, Economics and Social Choice,* by Victor R. Fuchs.

It is a real question, and it is part of the reason that the issue of proper care for the homeless matters so much. It is, without being dramatic about it, a matter of life and death. Unfed, the homeless starve. Unsheltered, they die of the cold. Funneled into shelters and hotels which are overcrowded and undersupervised, they get robbed, they get raped, they die in accidents. They get beaten to death.

No one even knows how bad it is, and yet it grows worse. This society, with all its computers and all its enormous wealth of resources and research, cannot count the homeless. Without addresses, telephone numbers or steady places of employment, they float, from soup kitchen to shelter, from season to season, from north to south and east to west, observed in passing but untracked.

The Reagan Administration has estimated their number at 250,000 to 300,000. Advocates for the homeless, angered by that, have guessed the population at two-and-a-half to three million. It is a ten-fold difference, and no one knows. Clearly, however, as we look about, it grows.

In late 1986, as the Atlanta business community advanced a plan to establish a "safeguard" zone downtown free of the litter of rheumy, panhandling derelict men who were haunting its doors, winter arrived. A lonely old man named William Casey lay down that night in a park in a very good neighborhood close in to town, and having had too much to drink, and clothes too thin, quietly died.

A year later, on the first freezing night of the winter of 1987 in Atlanta, three people died. Two were older men like Mr. Casey, stilled by hypothermia as they slept out in the open. But the third male who died, in a fire in a shelter, was Nicholas Paul Burke, aged 23 months, and the small white casket he was buried in, two weeks before Thanksgiving, was a sad little symptom of a disturbing progression.

If the traditional image of homelessness was that of wandering alcoholic men like Jimmy-the-Indian and Mr. Casey, the silhouette which stamped the last decade as different became that of the bag lady. She was the symbol of the hundreds of thousands of mentally ill people released from institutions beginning in the 1960's. Too frequently, they were released from warehouse care into a condition of no care at all, and many of them were severely mentally ill. In New York City, the Human Resources Administration has estimated that one-quarter of all shelter residents have a history of mental disorder. Similar estimates have been made in Boston, Washington, and other major cities.

They were people who were to have been helped by release, who were to have been treated as outpatients in community health centers and allowed to lead independent lives. But there was no suitable housing identified and waiting for them when they got out, or any program of job training, and the pattern of treatment never emerged. The community health centers which did develop were not equipped or inclined to deal with the severely mentally ill. Society didn't follow through.

The same accusation can be made in the case of veterans, particularly veterans of Viet Nam. Many of them never recovered from the experience. They were the next group to swell the ranks of the homeless, and many of them are emotionally crippled. Assessed one way in the vast and shadowed interior of the homeless condition, they number among the mentally ill. Counted another away, they are simply homeless veterans. In Los Angeles alone, the Homeless Veterans Division has estimated that there are 35,000 to 50,000 homeless people on the streets of the county, that half of them are veterans, and that half of those veterans served in Viet Nam. However they are counted, they aren't really helped.

And there are so many categories. There are families like Laura Santiago's, who have always been poor, but whose parents migrated two generations ago from Puerto Rico, in her case, or from the American south, in the case of many black families. The parents found work and cheap housing in states like New Jersey and New York, and many of their children, burdened with too many children of their own, and caught between soaring rents and increased competition for low-paying jobs, have become completely the creatures of the welfare system and its bizarre results. These, frequently, are the people for whom New York pays $1,000 to $2,500 a month in rent, to house families of four or five or six in hotel rooms 14 or 16 feet square, year after year.

The dignity and discipline of some of the people living day by day, raising children hour by hour in the violence of those places, amid drugs, fires, beatings, burglaries, prostitution and murder has to be witnessed to be appreciated. The pioneer spirit and determination of families who spurn the system, hacking and hammering homes out of abandoned buildings as the early colonists did out of the forests, has to be seen first-hand to be believed.

One needs to travel the country to get a physical sense of how broad the scope of homelessness in all its categories has become, how truly national the condition is, how helpful local volunteer efforts can be, but how dearly we lack an effective national plan of help.

In Lafayette, Louisiana one can find women who have been driven from their homes by batterings, by sexual abuse and rape, by strangers or by their husbands. One can find them there because there is a place in Lafayette for them to run to, a caring refuge founded by a determined group of women in the Roman Catholic community. But the victims who turn up there are from Detroit or Fort Lauderdale or Texas as well as from Louisiana. The victims are from everywhere.

In a potter's field in the desert outside Phoenix, Arizona on Thanksgiving Eve, in the headlights of a circle of cars, a crowd of the homeless and their advocates sang "Amazing Grace" in memory of the 121 homeless people who had died in Phoenix the previous 12 months. People from north, south, east and west. Because it is possible to survive the winter without heat in that climate, there are hundreds, if not thousands, of homeless people from all over the nation encamped in and around Phoenix in the cold months of the year.

And the most striking feature today about the homeless population in Phoenix, as in the nation, is the increasing number of families within it.

There are families with children, and some of them, camped in the desert outside town, are convinced they would starve if "Preacher Don" Deming, a retired master sergeant turned evangelical, didn't bring prayers and canned goods out to them each Sunday. Out there amongst the sagebrush and mesquite are men who don't shave because they can't afford razors, men without watches or clocks or any idea what time it is, families with nothing to put away for their next meal. Without a telephone, a car, an address, a clean body or clothes, it is impossible to get steady work. "Ninety-eight percent of the population in the United States doesn't even understand that this exists," the preacher said, rationing out his cans.

Many of those families had come looking for jobs. That is why Nicholas Burke was born in Atlanta. His parents, Mike and Anne, had moved there from Syracuse, New York, to try to find work. And he died in Atlanta because his father was trapped in the cycle of frustration common to unskilled workers today. In a service economy of minimum wage jobs and negligible benefits, they earn very little, and live just one illness or one layoff away from losing their telephone, their electricity, their car or their apartment.

The Burkes went from apartment to relatives to shelter and out again. They were in a sort of shelter-rooming house when the night turned cold, a blanket ignited on an electric heater, and Nickie died in a quick, intense fire.

Only then did some of the relatives they had left behind in the search for work learn how hard the Burkes of this country have to struggle to get along in America today.

"I only saw my grandson once in his short life when he was seven months old, for three days," the boy's paternal grandmother wrote in a letter to the people of Atlanta the week before Thanksgiving. "Please," she said, "remember the poor and homeless."

—DUDLEY CLENDINEN

PHOTOGRAPHY

The photography of HOMELESS IN AMERICA: A PHOTOGRAPHIC PROJECT was created on assignment by five photojournalists selected for the project at its inception. The work of these photographers, whose brief biographies follow below, was augmented with another collection of work gathered by HOMELESS IN AMERICA editors through a nationwide search for existing black and white images of homelessness across the United States. Seven student photojournalists also submitted work created during summer internships with the project. We are extremely grateful to these contributing photographers, who are credited in other portions of the book.

MARY ELLEN MARK began her first long-term photographic project in Turkey in 1965 with a Fulbright Fellowship and also focused on the problems of drug addiction in England and women in a maximum security ward at Oregon State Mental Hospital in her early career. Ms. Mark's 17-year photographic project in India has resulted in two books, one on prostitutes on Falkland Road in Bombay (*Falkland Road*, 1981) and Mother Theresa and her Missions of Charity. She has received Robert F. Kennedys Journalism Awards for this work and for her photographs of runaway children. Ms. Mark co-produced a film on runaways in Seattle with Martin Bell, *Streetwise*, which was nominated for an Academy Award for documentary feature series in 1985. Her picture agency is Archive in New York City, where she currently resides.

BILL PIERCE has a 20-year photographic career with a reputation for sensitive coverage of the socially disadvantaged. He was awarded the Overseas Press Club award for best photoreportage from Beiruit and Northern Ireland covering the Children of War. A photojournalist, lecturer and writer, Mr. Pierce's work has been published in *A Day in the Life of Japan; War Torn: Survivors and Victims of the Late 20th Century;* and *A Day in the Life of America;* it is also included in the permanent collections of the National Portrait Gallery and the Corcoran Gallery of Art. His photographs have appeared widely in world magazines, from *LIFE* and *TIME* to *Paris Match* and *Stern,* among others. Mr. Pierce is a contract photographer for *TIME Magazine* and lives in New York City.

ELI REED began his career at the *Detroit News* in 1978 and then moved to the *San Francisco Examiner* in 1980, where he was a Pulitzer Prize finalist for his coverage of a housing project for lower income residents. In 1982, Mr. Reed was awarded a Nieman Fellowship and won the Overseas Press Club Award for best photoreportage for newspapers and wire services. His book of color photography on the survival of the city of Beiruit will be published this spring. Mr. Reed is affiliated with Magnum Photos, Inc. and lives in New York City.

EUGENE RICHARDS' first book, *Few Comforts or Surprises: The Arkansas Delta* was published in 1973 and led to his founding of Many Voices Press and Voices Gallery to encourage documentary photography through exhibitions and lectures. Mr. Richards' three most recent works include *Fifty Hours* (1983), a project on emergency room medicine; *Exploding into Life* (1986), an inspirational diary in words and pictures of Dorothea Lynch's fatal battle with cancer; and *Below the Line: Poverty in the United States* (1987). Mr. Richards has received the W. Eugene Smith Award, a Guggenheim Fellowhip and an NEA grant for his work. He was awarded the International Center for Photography Photographer of the Year award in 1987. Mr. Richards is affiliated with Magnum Photos, Inc. and lives in New York City.

STEPHEN SHAMES began his documentary work with photographic essays on cocaine abuse and child poverty, for which he received two Robert F. Kennedy Journalism Awards and the NPPA Photographer of the Year Award for Excellence. He has spent the past nine years documenting the problems of poor children in America, and included in this work are essays on child prostitution in Times Square; runaways on Interstate 5; and street children living in an abandoned building in the Bronx (an 8-year project). Mr. Shames received an Alicia Patterson Fellowship in 1985 to continue his documentary work on poor children and their families. He is currently on leave from the *Philadelphia Inquirer* while he continues this work.

JIM HUBBARD began his career at the *Detroit News* in 1966, then photographed news for United Press International from 1969 to 1986. During this time he won National Press Photographer Association and White House News Photographer Association awards for a variety of picture stories ranging from the Indian takeover at Wounded Knee and the Detroit riots to the Olympic massacre at Munich in 1972. Mr. Hubbard has been photographing poverty issues, and homelessness in particular, since 1982. He lives in Washington, D.C.

Darkness has not path
nor matter to touch.
Blindly you walk in to it
hoping to meet no obstacles.
The further you walk
the more lost you become.

You look back
and don't know how far
you have gone
you look ahead
and don't know how far
you have to go.

You hear noises
but you can't see anything.
You become afraid.
Fear of not knowing
Creates panic in your heart.

For some reason, you go on.
You hope there's an end.
A place of light.
A place where you're not alone.
Time has no meaning,
but you hope to get there soon.

Poem found in abandoned tent
Burlington, Vermont
July 1987

Burlington, Vermont, August 1987
BILL PIERCE

Sacramento, California, August 1987
GARY POWELL

Train Station, Hartford, Connecticut, June 1986
PHIL FARNSWORTH

Los Angeles, June 1987
RONALD CORBIN

Man with no socks.
New York City, February 1985
NANCY MILLER ELLIOTT

Robert Cox holds photograph of family. He died January 1987 during a snowstorm.
Washington, D.C., October 1986
Jerome Friar

New York City, June 1986
ABRAHAM MENASHE

Mount Holly, New Jersey, August 1987
Kim Weimer

John Carlton. Died August 1985.
New York City, January 1985
NANCY MILLER ELLIOTT

What I know about being homeless is this. In New Jersey it snows in the winter so you have to find some shelter or die. I know about these nasal inhalers, this is the product you use to clear up your nose. If you break open the plastic container there is a cotton swab inside if you swallow this swab the ingredients speed up your metabolism so you are able to stay awake all night and not fall asleep in the snow and die.

So I started eating these nasal inhalers. I may have eaten 5-10,000 of them. I lived under bridges in Salvation Army boxes, anywhere I could. It is a miracle that I am alive because these inhalers are very powerful. Living on the street can be very hard. It can also be very rewarding because street people are very caring and loving people who will share with you if they see you are really in need. But it is a vicious cycle you can not get a job because you do not have an address you do not have an address because you do not have any money, you do not have any money because you do not have a job. As this process continues your self esteem and self confidence slowly ebb away. So most people who are living on the street have given up knowing any other way of life.

Fortunately for me God and his son Jesus Christ and the Holy Spirit were with me the whole time and they saved my life.

— Danny Cahill

Exerpted from the book
Forgotten Voices, Unforgettable Dreams,
edited by Deborah Mashibini

Reprinted by permission of the author.

Metro Station, Washington, D.C., October 1987
TONEE HARBERT

New York City, June 1986
ABRAHAM MENASHE

Acquilla Tignor lives with her family under an overpass.
Long Beach, California, September 1987
AXEL KOESTER

Darcy & Andrew
Bible Tabernacle Mission, Venice, California, October 1987
MARY ELLEN MARK

Paula & Verenis
Valley Shelter, North Hollywood, California, October 1987
MARY ELLEN MARK

Linda Avalas & son Shaun
Valley Shelter, North Hollywood, California, October 1987
MARY ELLEN MARK

Shirley Sertain & Matthew Sertain
Gilbert Hotel, Hollywood, California, October 1987
MARY ELLEN MARK

Cathleen Hamm & son Michael
Bible Tabernacle Mission, Venice, California, October 1987
MARY ELLEN MARK

"Bear," "Angel" and Angelique
Hollywood, California, October 1987
MARY ELLEN MARK

Humane Society removing family pets during eviction.
Social service workers arrived a half-day later for the family.
Alexandria, Virginia, August 1987
JIM HUBBARD

Christ House: transitional housing three months following eviction.
Alexandria, Virginia, October 1987
JIM HUBBARD

Eviction: the Fitzgerald family.
Alexandria, Virginia, August 1987
JIM HUBBARD

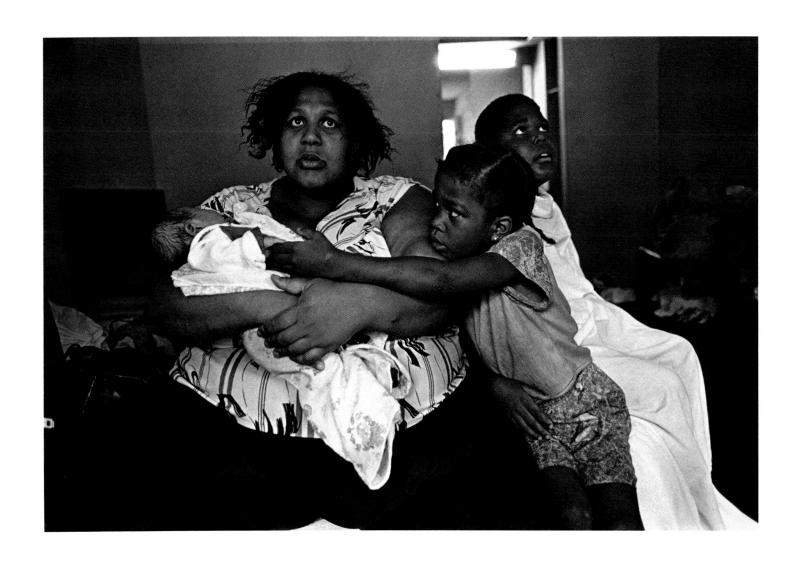

Awaiting eviction, July Fourth weekend. Liberty Motor Inn.
North Bergen, New Jersey
July 1987
EUGENE RICHARDS

Families and belongings outside of Liberty Motor Inn.
North Bergen, New Jersey, July 1987
EUGENE RICHARDS

Jeannette and William Corvan after eviction from the Liberty Motor Inn.
North Bergen, New Jersey, July 1987
EUGENE RICHARDS

Jeanette and William Corvan at their new home, a vacant lot across from the Liberty Motor Inn.
North Bergen, New Jersey, July 1987
Eugene Richards

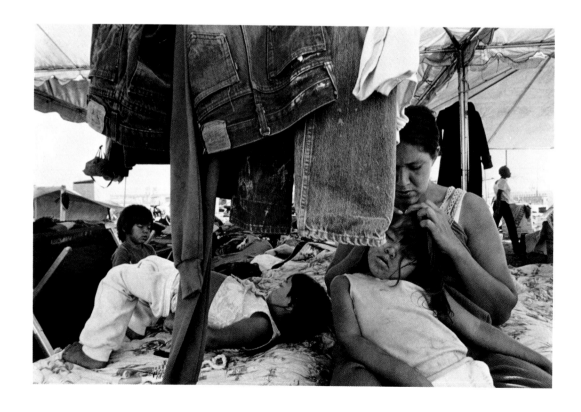

Opposite and above:
Urban campground for the homeless ("Tent City") in Los Angeles.
August 1987
EUGENE RICHARDS

Opposite and above:
"Tent City" Los Angeles
August 1987
EUGENE RICHARDS

Cleveland Taylor O'Neill, 68. Asheville-Buncombe Community Christian Ministry Shelter.
Asheville, North Carolina, August 1987
Loup Langton

Temporary camps are regularly bulldozed.
Santa Barbara, California, January 1987
EVE FOWLER

47

Melvia Clay with son and daughter. Hamilton Church Shelter.
San Francisco, California, September 1987
SIBYLLA HERBRICH

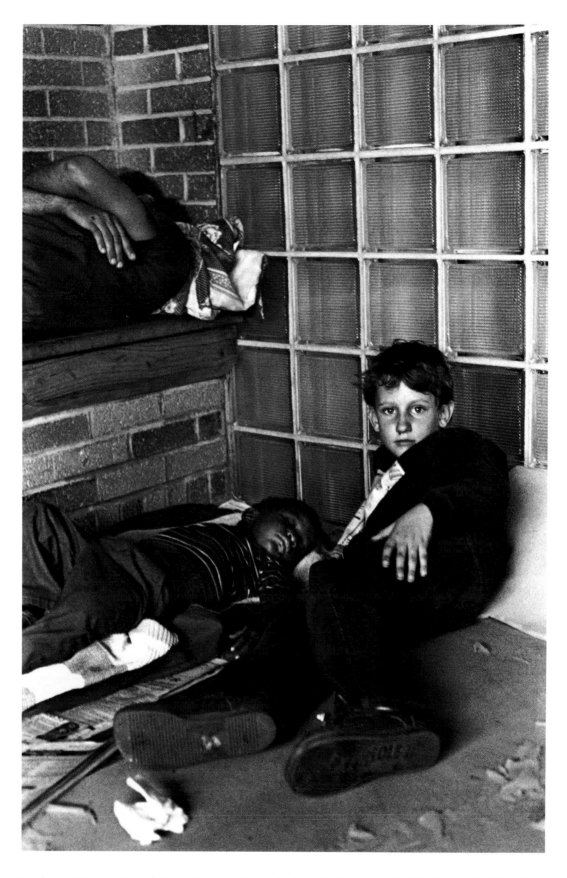

Randrique Norman, 2, and Aaron Burgess, 7, outside the Saint Vincent de Paul Shelter for the Homeless.
Dayton, Ohio, September 1987
GRACE WOJDA

Battered woman with children.
St. Louis, Missouri, July 1987
ELI REED

Near Hudson River.
New York City, July 1986
WILLIAM VIGGIANO

Pat Beck, Bucks County Campground.
Bucks County, Pennsylvania, September 1987
STEPHEN SHAMES/*The Philadelphia Inquirer*

Germaine and Rick Haraschak have full-time jobs and three children. Bucks County Campground.
Bucks County, Pennsylvania, October 1987
STEPHEN SHAMES/*The Philadelphia Inquirer*

Beck family asleep in car.
Bucks County, Pennsylvania, September 1987
STEPHEN SHAMES/*The Philadelphia Inquirer*

Family Dispute: David and Kay O'Connell with daughter Kelly, 5. George Washington Motel.
Bucks County, Pennsylvania, September 1987
STEPHEN SHAMES/*The Philadelphia Inquirer*

Bathtub playground. Holland Hotel.
New York City, October 1987
STEPHEN SHAMES

Toni Hall washing dishes. Holland Hotel.
New York City, October 1987
STEPHEN SHAMES

Vanessa Spencer and her children. Holland Hotel.
New York City, September 1987
STEPHEN SHAMES

Max kisses his sister Vanessa. Holland Hotel.
New York City, October 1987
STEPHEN SHAMES

Children at play. Holland Hotel.
New York City, October 1987
STEPHEN SHAMES

Ronald Singletary
"I don't want my kids in here. It's the atmosphere. It's nothing for no kids to see.
It will affect them the rest of their lives."
Holland Hotel
New York City, October 1987
STEPHEN SHAMES

New Life Evangelical Women's Shelter
East St. Louis, Missouri, July 1987
ELI REED

PUBLIC STARECASE

My stare quota's about up
So don't mess with me today

I have been stared at while I waited on the soup line
(by someone who had time
        in a car:
    stopped at the light:
    whipped out a camera:
        smiled and split)
(Photos all neat and tucked away in a
    scrapbook now
excursion from suburbia —
'ah i got a live one…just like you see in the daily news

Well I was stared at at my locker
(learned as I have to deftly sort
        laundry
        books
        papers
        pens
        frustrations
        petitions
        ministrations
        admissions
all in a 5 minute moment
as commuters gawk their button-down gawk or
blankly vacate their bodies past
    to where their eyes and heart slipped years before
vacant stares

judgement oozes uncontained in silence
    from those eyes and
I feel all at once violated, stripped, exposed
I'm angry now: fighting mad but
    broken and
        crushed as a tiny powerless child
        feeling shame
just from those stares
just in a fleeting moment
I blush the pain of shame
    being caught in private things
        in public
the private is just my life
    exposed   forced to live in public
hide as I may

When we're together
    brothers and sisters tossed remnant of a homed society
it's easier: bantering, joking
    provoking and stroking
so it doesn't feel so raw
I feel raw now

It seems only anger will rev up the energy
    to hold on tight to me
because though they (*they,* I say: the homed)
    fear us
I want you to know *they* will eat *us* alive.
bit by bit
they chew our lives and
        spit it out digested in lies
    running 300 words under explosive headlines
the press spitoon

They design us; re-design us and assign us
    through The System
all the while eating us alive
        with their locked church doors and forced vanning
frightening shelters and refusal to extend one blanket

they are eating us alive while leaving us to starve
and I tell you —
    those stares?
        they are inviting us to dinner

—Annie Q.

Exerpted from the book
Forgotten Voices, Unforgettable Dreams
edited by Deborah Mashibini

Reprinted by permission of the author.

New York City, September 1987
MAUREEN FENNELLI

Hollywood Boulevard alley
Hollywood, California, October 1987
MARY ELLEN MARK

"Pagan", 16, runaway from Arizona
Hollywood, California, November 1987
MARY ELLEN MARK

Maddy Fetten, Skid Row Women's Shelter
Los Angeles, October 1987
MARY ELLEN MARK

"Shadow", 18, blind at birth
Hollywood, California, November 1987
MARY ELLEN MARK

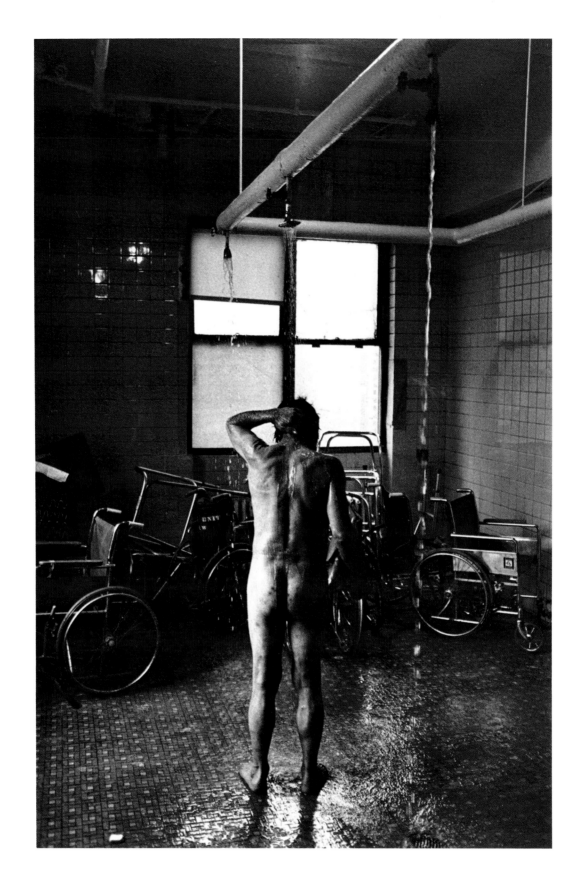

Shelter for homeless men
New York City, August 1985
GEORGE COHEN

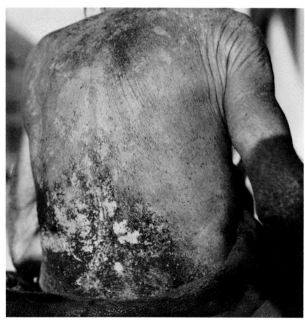

"I feel like I have tumors all over my body."
Los Angeles, September 1987
DON WEINSTEIN

Naples, Florida, August 1987
EUGENE RICHARDS

Naples, Florida, August 1987
EUGENE RICHARDS

"Well, Kentucky Fried, about 1:00 they throw it out. After breakfast. McDonald's is the same way…sometimes, you'll eat out of those dumpsters, that'll make you sick. What it is, tears your stomach up. Sometimes you get ahold of some bad meat…"
Naples, Florida, August 1987
EUGENE RICHARDS

Living under the streets
St. Louis, Missouri, July 1987
ELI REED

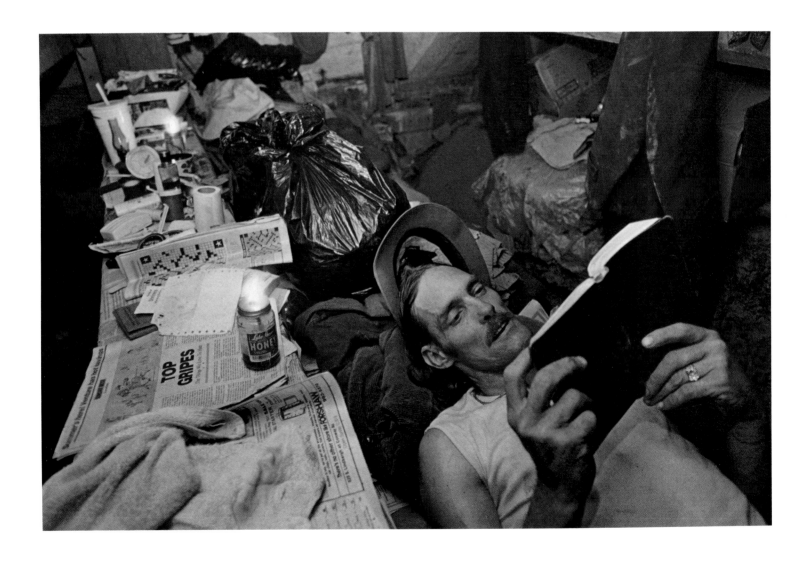

Bible Study
St. Louis, Missouri, July 1987
ELI REED

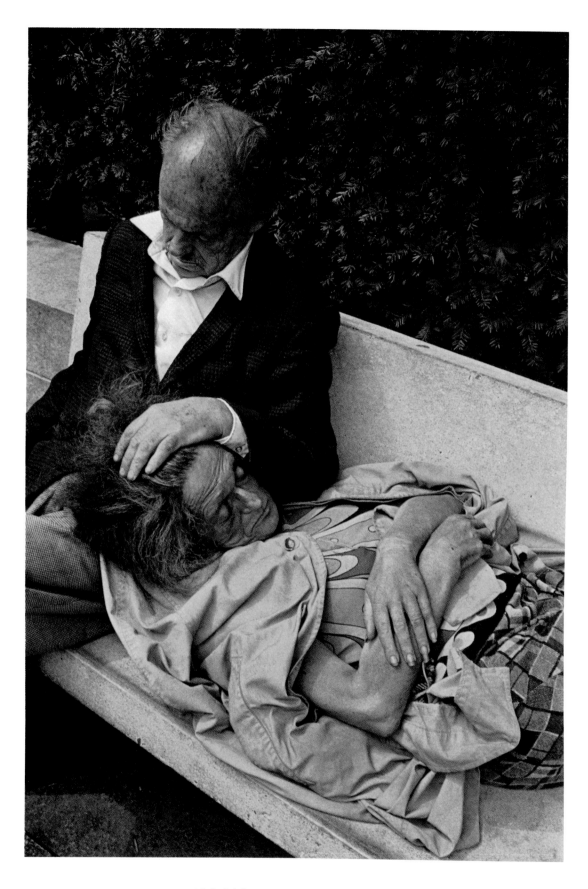

Philadelphia, Pennsylvania, July 1986
JAMES CONROY

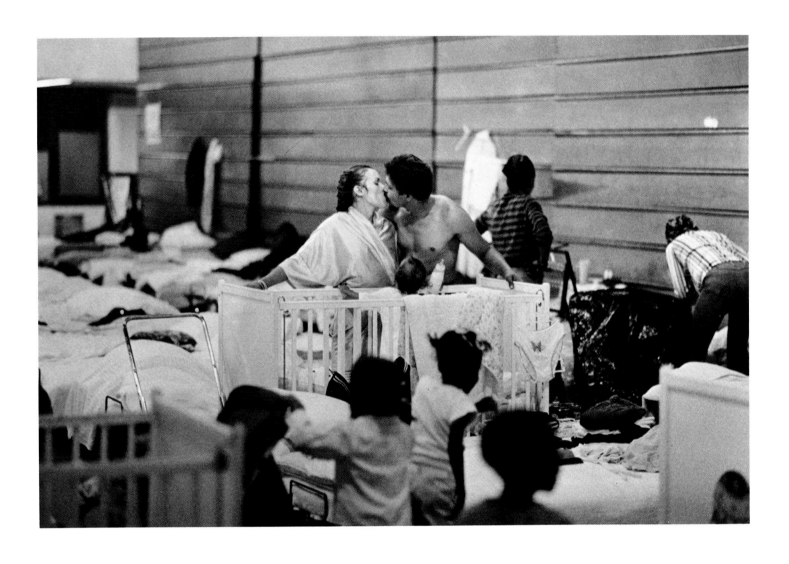

Roberto Clemente State park gymnasium, serving as a New York City shelter for homeless families
June 1985
GEORGE COHEN

Food Line
Dallas, Texas, August 1987
MICHAEL D. JOHNSON

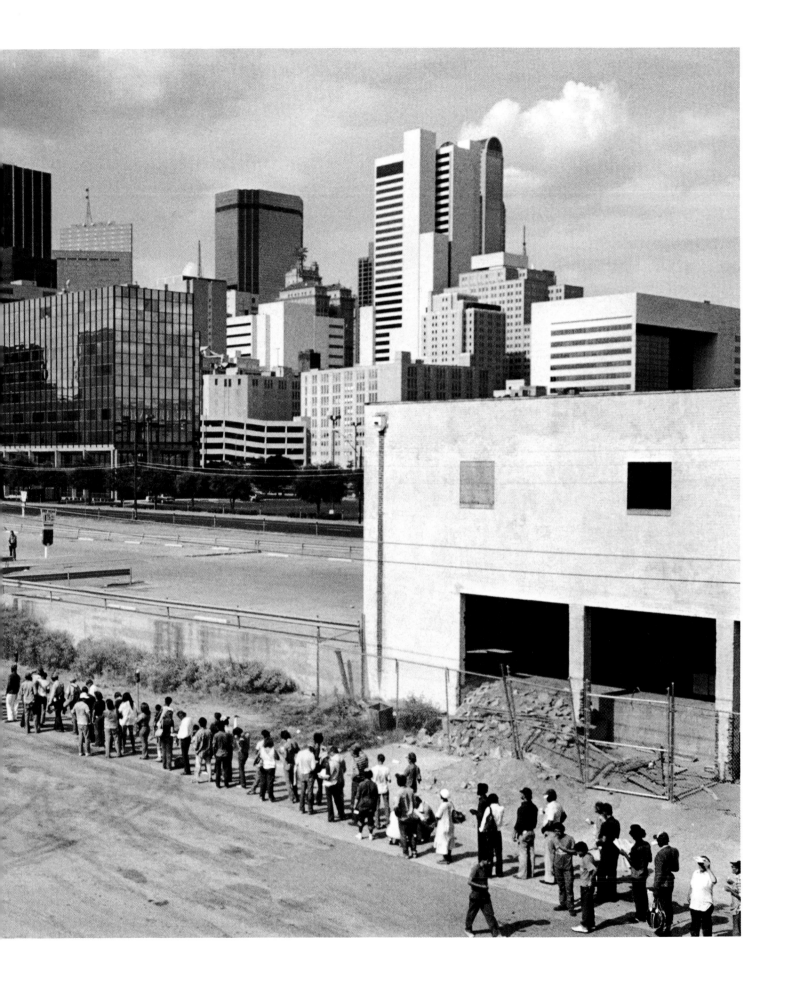

Houston, Texas, April 1985
ROBB KENDRICK

Mercedes Cardona, Brooklyn Arms Hotel
New York City, October 1987
STEPHEN SHAMES

New Life Evangelical Women's Shelter
East St. Louis, Missouri, July 1987
ELI REED

Life under an overpass
Hartford, Connecticut, June 1986
PHIL FARNSWORTH

A WOMAN ALONE

So many dreams and wishes passed by. What were the dreams
my mother had for me as she gazed down on her first
born — Would she approve of the direction my life has taken?

Have you had this plan all along, to allow me to be tested
and pulled almost to the breaking point? Dead, but not
dying — bruised, but not broken?

What about me Lord? Don't you care?

I know how it feels to face death and yet live, with my
friends watching to see if I would live or die while they
safely peeked through the curtains.

I see others with husbands, fathers, even a family — do they
feel alone in a way different than I?

Is this my training ground to break a trail to a new and
different place — where only faith abounds?

Let me feel peace in spite of the problems people see around
me. Give me the faith not always to look back but to live
this day to the fullest. That when the hearing or the sight
fail or when the shaking starts not be ashamed, for
others don't know how I got this way.

I have longed for a friend to talk with who can understand.
Don't let me hold the violence and hurt too close to me that
I don't let anyone in.

If I am sick and bruised and have nowhere to go for a warm
meal, a blanket, an encouraging word — do I have a right to
wonder why?

— June Williams

who travels with husband Gordon
ministering to other homeless individuals
and families across the West.

June Williams
Sacramento, California, September 1987
GARY POWELL

SOME
RESPONSES TO
HOMELESSNESS

WOMEN OF HOPE

PHOTOGRAPHS BY STEPHEN SHAMES

Women of Hope was founded to address the needs of chronically mentally ill homeless women of Philadelphia, Pennsylvania. Program Director Sister Mary Scullion explains, "Many times precisely because of their mental and physical disabilities, these women were discriminated against by social service agencies and shelters; because they heard voices, because they wouldn't take showers daily. Our program is designed to care for their particular needs. We take everything slowly, one day at a time. We also follow the cases through, because releasing the mentally ill from any shelter without follow-up means return to the streets."

At first, neighbors were skeptical, Sister Mary says — Would the shelter attract more homeless? Would it drive property values down? Bring disruption into the neighborhood? But over the past two and a half years, the area Neighborhood Advisory Board has worked to understand the program, to integrate the program into the community. Property values have gone up and Women of Hope receives donations of money and volunteer time. People who live in the area have been supportive.

"Our greatest problem centers around the myth of mental illness. When most people look at the homeless on the streets, the mentally ill homeless, they look completely crazy — mentally and physically hopeless. Like they should be put in mental institutions. Our experience has been that even the most resistant, the most ill individual will come off the streets and accept physical and mental health care. Sometimes it takes a short period of hospitalization and special care to get the physical problems under control (diabetes, arthritis, frostbite). Then we begin to work on breaking the cycle of homelessness through therapy, counseling."

On average, nine of every ten women who've left Women of Hope have broken what Sister Mary calls "the cycle of homelessness." Some are back with their families, a few have gotten apartments with social services, some have moved to boarding houses, to YMCA's or other single-room occupancy, or SRO, places. "What works best is treating people like human beings, taking it slow," the sister says. "It's a long process. We encourage self-determination. These are all interesting people — they have gifts as well as disabilities — and they can contribute to the life of the community. One woman at our shelter is a great cook; one's working as a receptionist; several are working with a city project to organize the mentally ill. The homeless need access to quality physical and mental care that is responsive to their needs. They need SRO's, foster families, low income housing — a variety of options."

Here and there, on the Lower East Side of New York, there are semi-official looking signs posted on the fronts of buildings whose gaping windows and crumbling fronts mark them as abandoned by their owners, left by the city. "This Land Is Ours. Property of the People of the Lower East Side. Not For Sale." In those old apartment buildings, and in many others without the militant signs, are homeless people who have made homes in property no one else is using. They have no regular jobs or they have jobs which do not pay them enough for a room or apartment. They are single. They are men and women living together. Many are families with children. They are squatters. Spurning the city's bureaucracy, its chaotic shelter system, and its cramped and dangerous welfare hotels, they choose instead to homestead in the dark and shattered interior spaces of these abandoned buildings. Some simply crawl in and crawl out, making a rude nest. Others hammer and saw, wire and plumb, making extensive improvements, creating an orderly environment, hopeful that the city will be impressed by their commitment and will cede title to them. "The city would rather pay $1700 a month for us to stay in a welfare hotel. They think I'm better off in a welfare hotel, and for me that's foolishness," says Laura Santiago, 40. She and her husband and son Eduardo Jr., 7, are in their third abandoned building. The first one burned. They had to sleep under sheets of plywood and umbrellas because it had no roof. In this one they have rebuilt an apartment from scraps of construction trash and what sheetrock they could afford. They live on welfare and day labor. They carry water up the stairs from the fire hydrant. They divert electricity from a Consolidated Edison pole. They and other inhabitants have a house committee and rules, she said, "like no drugs, no violence, no stealing." They put everything they have into making the apartment better, and live with the same worry that nags all squatters. "What if the city turns around and says we're knocking the building down or we're going to take it away from you?" she asks.

She cannot afford a newspaper, but someone showed her a copy of a story in the Daily News that said the city might try to evict the squatters in the spring. It worries her. It angers John DeFalco, who works as a messenger and lives on top of a nearby building he has labored to restore. They won't let the city take their building, even if it takes a fight. "We'll get out of jail and come back and open the building," he promised. "This is home, man!"

SQUATTERS

PHOTOGRAPHS BY STEPHEN SHAMES

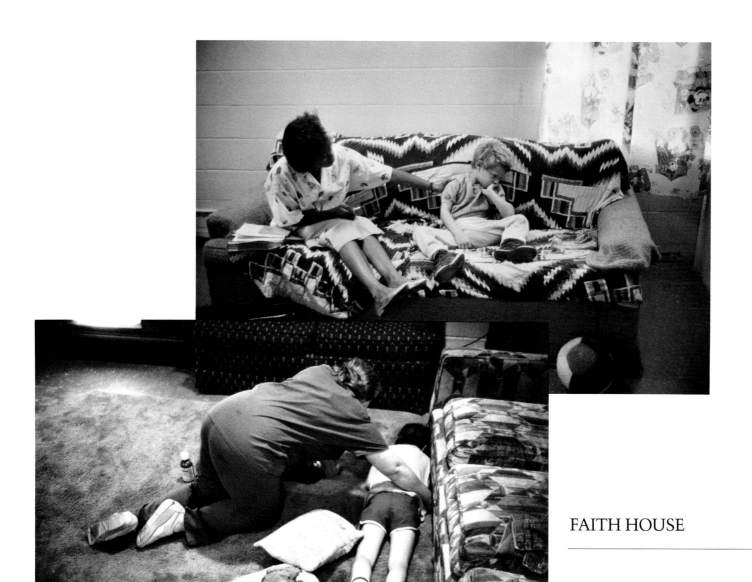

FAITH HOUSE

As with some corporations, and even some nations, some programs of care for the homeless grow from the faith and vision of one person who inspires or maneuvers or simply exhausts others into cooperating and contributing, so that an organizational base is built, and needs begin to be met, and then a larger structure of support is built on that base, until it becomes plain to all that the program is working and people are being served. And at that point, larger institutions and levels of government find it hard not to support the program with church charity or local tax monies or federal grants.

In Lafayette, in southern Louisiana, the person who founded Faith House Emergency Shelter for Women in 1980 was Sister Marie Thomas. Lafayette is Cajun country, an area of extended families, strongly Roman Catholic and socially traditional. It is a felt community, and the Sister knew her network. "She talked in all the Catholic churches," said Marcelle Citron, president of Faith House. "One man has given us over $30,000. He said, 'That little nun could have sold rusty nails'." The sister has since died, and in the collapse of the petroleum economy in Louisiana, banks, res-

taurants, motels and all sorts of businesses failed in Lafayette. But Mrs. Citron is indomitable. "There is no reason to want for anything in this town," she insists. She has made Faith House a community project.

Brother Christian Rountree and Sister Mercedes Couvillion have done the same thing with the St. Joseph Diner and the St. Joseph Shelter for Men. Women's clubs, restaurants, beauty parlors, dentists, pediatricians, supermarkets and churches all give goods and services. The diner feeds 150 to 250 people at noon each day with food donated by 18 different stores, and cooked by volunteers from 20 different churches. After seven years of operation, sheltering and counseling hundreds of homeless and battered women, Faith House last fall was able to qualify for $22,500 in federal HUD money distributed through the city, as was the men's shelter. Faith House was then feeding, sheltering and counseling 13 women and 13 children at a monthly cost of only slightly more than twice what New York City was paying to house a family of five in one room of the Brooklyn Arms Hotel.

PHOTOGRAPHS BY STEPHEN SHAMES

HOW YOU CAN HELP

We must create long-term solutions to homelessness to prevent homelessness from becoming an American institution.

The following organizations and agencies can help you take action by providing more information on homelessness, identifying opportunities to volunteer, and offering ideas and strategies for private individuals and corporations interested in working toward permanent solutions.

NATIONAL ORGANIZATIONS

State and local chapters of the organizations listed below can direct you to specific programs in your area.

American Red Cross
17th & D Streets, NE
Washington, DC 20006
202/639-3610

Committee for Food and Shelter
1518 K Street, NW/Suite 206
Washington, DC 20005
202/638-1526

Council of Jewish Federations
227 Massachusetts Avenue, NE
Washington, DC 20002
202/547-0200

National Coalition for the Homeless
105 East 22nd Street
New York, NY 10010
212/460-8110
or

1439 Rhode Island Avenue, NW
Washington, DC 20005
202/659-3310
or
311 South Spring Street, Suite 520
Los Angeles, CA 90013
213/488-9137

Catholic Charities U.S.A.
1319 F Street, NW
Fourth Floor
Washington, DC 20004
202/639-8400

National Council of Churches of
  Christ in the U.S.A.
110 Maryland Avenue, NE
Washington, DC 20002
202/544-2350

National Mental Health Association
1021 Prince Street
Alexandria, VA 22314-2971
703/684-7722

Salvation Army
1025 Vermont Avenue, NW
Washington, DC 20005
202/639-8414

United Conference of Mayors
1620 Eye Street, NW
Washington, DC 20006
202/293-7330

United Way of America
701 North Fairfax Street
Alexandria, VA 22314
703/836-7100

CLEARINGHOUSES ON HOMELESSNESS

Several national clearinghouses offer information and technical assistance on programs for homeless individuals or maintain lists of local opportunities for individuals to volunteer.

The Homeless Information Exchange
1120 G Street, NW
Suite 900
Washington, DC 20005
202/628-2990

National Volunteer Clearinghouse for the Homeless
1310 Emerson Street, NW
Washington, DC 20011
202/722-2740
1-800-HELP-664 (outside Washington, DC)

The Clearinghouse on Homelessness Among
Mentally Ill People
8630 Fenton Street
Silver Spring, MD 20901
301/588-5484

FEDERAL AGENCIES

Congress has created several Federal Agencies to assist homeless individuals, many of which have state and local programs in action.

Health Resources and Services Administration
Health Care for the Homeless
Parklawn Building, Room 7A 55
5600 Fishers Lane
Rockville, MD 20857
301/443-4220

National Institute of Mental Health
   Program for the Homeless Mentally Ill
Parklawn Building, Room 11C-25
5600 Fishers Lane
Rockville, MD 20857
301/443-3706

National Institute on Alcohol Abuse and Alcoholism
Community Demonstration Projects for Alcohol and
   Drug Abuse
Treatment for Homeless Individuals
Parklawn Building, Room 16C-02
5600 Fishers Lane
Rockville, MD 20857
301/443-1284

U.S. Department of Education
Education of Homeless Children and Youth
400 Maryland Avenue, SW Room 4073
Washington, DC 20202
202/732-4682

U.S. Department of Housing and Urban Development
Transitional Housing
Office of Elderly and Assisted Housing
451 7th Street, SW, Room 7282
Washington, DC 20410-8000
202/755-9075

U.S. Department of Housing and Urban Development
Emergency Shelter Grant Program for the Homeless
Entitlement Cities Division and Block Grant
   Assistance
451 7th Street, SW
Washington, DC 20410-8000
202/755-5977

U.S. Department of Labor
Job Training for the Homeless
Office of Strategy Planning and Policy Development
Employment and Training Administration
200 Constitution Avenue, NW, Room N-5637
Washington, DC 20210
202/535-0659

Veterans Medical Center
50 Irving Street, NW
Washington, DC 20422
202/745-8000
(Programs for homeless veterans are in operation in VA hospitals across the country.)

CONGRESS

Write to or call your Senators and Representatives in Congress and urge them to press for legislation to assist the homeless.

The names of your Senators and Representatives are available at your local library. Address your letters as follows:

Senator:
The Honorable
United States Senate
Washington, DC 20510

Representative:
The Honorable
U.S. House of Representatives
Washington, DC 20515

You can also call your Senators and Representatives by telephoning the Capitol Switchboard at 202/224-3121.

Washington, D.C.
October 1987
Michael O'Brien

AFTERWORD

"Homeless in America: A Photographic Project" is a cooperative private-sector venture that seeks to raise the level of public awareness and concern over the plight of America's homeless population. It is the brainchild of Susan Baker, Tipper Gore, Elizabeth Wallace and Janet Waxman, who founded Families for the Homeless.

Homelessness is so pervasive in this country that no book could serve as a definitive or all-encompassing treatment of the subject. Our attempt, over the course of a year, has been to illustrate the human dimensions of the problem.

We know that there is widespread disagreement about the number of homeless men, women and children in America, and even wider disagreement at all levels of government and society over how to help them.

But, our involvement with this project has led us to some conclusions.

First: Individual efforts in local communities do make a difference.

Second: Americans must make it clear to their elected representatives that homelessness is simply unacceptable. However, to attempt to eliminate homelessness without addressing its underlying causes, particularly the lack of low-income housing, will be an exercise in futility. Housing policies of the past, while well meant have not proven successful. New approaches must be made.

Third: Money in and of itself, whether from private sources or the public purse, is not enough. Money, in the absence of informed, thoughtful and comprehensive priorities and policies, will never be enough. More individual involvement in the political process itself and in the programs and institutions created is key.

Fourth: The incidence of homelessness is increasing rapidly, particularly among families and the employed.

There is a biblical admonition that any society is judged by its treatment of the least of its members. Some years ago, Pogo put it another way: "I have seen the enemy and it is us." Substitute "problem" for "enemy" and Pogo's point is one that we can still apply to ourselves.

Our once simple society, filled with a youthful confidence in the existence of easy answers and quick fixes, has evolved into a complex middle-aged society, filled with stress-inducing uncertainties. Withdrawal from the discomforts of these times has led to a surfeit of cynicism, conspicuous consumption — indeed, to the severe attenuation of our once strong sense of community. Fewer and fewer Americans even take the time to vote. "Not in my back yard" and "It's not my problem" have largely become the political response of latter-day America.

Most Americans feel with no small measure of justification that our society is the best in the world. However, the mere existence of the homeless, to say nothing of their rapidly swelling ranks, is a graphic reminder of how far our society still has to go. Just as we are now suffering the consequences of our past ecological excesses, will we wait until the streets of our cities resemble those of Calcutta before we address the situation in a truly meaningful way? It is the political fashion, in some circles, to attack national programs as unwieldy and wasteful. Democracy itself is untidy and inefficient. The complexities of dealing with homelessness ought not to deter us from action.

We need more photojournalism today in the tradition of Dorothea Lange, Jacob Riis and W. Eugene Smith. Those who work in the spirit of this great American tradition deserve more space and recognition. This project, which attempted to follow this tradition, could not have enjoyed any measure of success without the great contributions of time and effort from a host of interested, concerned and very talented individuals.

I would particularly like to thank:

The Governing Board of HOMELESS IN AMERICA: A PHOTOGRAPHIC PROJECT;

Nelson Peltz and Peter May of Triangle Industries, Inc., whose generosity and early commitment to this project was so critical, and Triangle's Manny Schultz and Jonas Halperin;

David Maxwell, Hugh Flaherty and Harriet Ivey of Fannie Mae; Glenn Ihrig of The Public Welfare Foundation, Inc. and Colby Chandler and Raymond DeMoulin of Eastman Kodak Company, for their timely and generous support;

Susie Elson, Past President, Preston Garrison, National Executive Director, and John Ambrose, Manager of Public Policy, of the National Mental Health Association;

Mary Ellen Mark, Bill Pierce, Eli Reed, Eugene Richards, Stephen Shames and Jim Hubbard for their months of extraordinary photojournalism on assignment across the country;

The other photographers who contributed thousands of photographs for use in the work, whose commitment to documentary photography I respect and admire;

The advisory panel which met with our staff at the start of our project: Ike Fields of the United Way and Joe France of the Red Cross; Sandra Brawders of the House of Ruth; and Irene Shifren-Levine of the National Institute of Mental Health;

Max Lent, of National Public Data, for data base information for the travelling exhibition;

For their great assistance in assignment photography, in Los Angeles: Teen Canteen, Para Los Ninos, Children of the Night, Angel's Flight, Valley Shelter Mission, Bible Tabernacle Mission, People and Progress, Skid Row Women's Shelter, the Salvation Army, The Oasis, Burbank Temporary Aid Center, Walter Contreras, Fred Jordan Mission; in Lafayette, Louisiana: Marcelle Citron and Jeannette Baggett of Faith House; in Philadelphia: Gene Roberts of the *Philadelphia Inquirer*, Sister Mary Scullion and Dion Martin of Women of Hope, Laura van Tosh of Project SHARE; in St. Louis: the New Life Evangelical Center; in New York City: Beth Gorey and the staff of the National Coalition for the Homeless and Ronald Singletary at the Holland Hotel; in Washington, D.C.: Judith Johnson at the Green Door; in Naples, Florida, Jeff Ryan; and Janine Altongy.

Alex and Caroline Castro for their inspired book and exibition design;

Phil Horton of the law firm of Arnold & Porter for his gently tenacious counsel;

Dudley Clendinen, for his eloquence and persistence;

Robin Smith, for her brilliant adaptation of our project to video;

Amy Whiteside, our gifted darkroom printer;

Edward Clift, our assiduous project intern;

Special thanks to Marjorie Brown and Katherine Glennon, my associate and assistant editors, who have struggled creatively and persistently through the long year with me to bring this project to light;

And Story Shem, Marthena Cowart and Karen Chamberlain at ARRIVE, whose belief, wise counsel and determination helped make the project possible.

MICHAEL EVANS
Washington, DC
December, 1987